Countries Around the World

Haiti

Elizabeth Raum

www.raintreepublishers.co.uk
Visit our website to find out
more information about
Raintree books.

To order:
☎ Phone 0845 6044371
🖷 Fax +44 (0) 1865 312263
🖳 Email myorders@raintreepublishers.co.uk

Customers from outside the UK please telephone +44 1865 312262

Raintree is an imprint of Capstone Global Library Limited,
a company incorporated in England and Wales having its
registered office at 7 Pilgrim Street, London, EC4V 6LB –
Registered company number: 6695582

Text © Capstone Global Library Limited 2012
First published in hardback in 2012
The moral rights of the proprietor have been asserted.

Edited by Louise Galpine and Megan Cotugno
Designed by Ryan Frieson
Original illustrations © Capstone Global Library, Ltd, 2012
Illustrated by Oxford Designers & Illustrators
Picture research by Tracy Cummins
Originated by Capstone Global Library, Ltd
Printed in China by China Translation and Printing Services

ISBN 978 1 406 22789 5 (hardback)
15 14 13 12 11
10 9 8 7 6 5 4 3 2 1

British Library Cataloguing in Publication Data
Raum, Elizabeth.
Haiti. -- (Countries around the world)
972.9'4073-dc22
A full catalogue record for this book is available from the
British Library.

Acknowledgements
We would like to thank the following for permission to
reproduce photographs: © age fotostock: p. 30 (© Blinkcatcher);
© Alamy: p. 25 (© Jan Sochor); © Corbis: pp. 7 (© The Gallery
Collection), 8 (© Bettmann), 13 (© Gideon Mendel), 21
(© Niko Guido), 24 (© Philip Gould), 28 (© Carlos Cazalis),
33(© ANDRES MARTINEZ CASARES/epa/); © Getty Images:
pp. 15 (YURI CORTEZ/AFP), 17 (Mario Tama), 23 (THONY
BELIZAIRE/AFP/), 33 (EITAN ABRAMOVICH/AFP), 35
(Joe Raedle); © istockphoto: pp. 5 (© Zach Wear), 11
(© Claudia Dewald); © National Geographic Stock: p. 9
(© JAMES P. BLAIR); © Photo Researchers: p. 18 (© Nicholas
Smythe); © Shutterstock: pp. 27 (© arindambanerjee), 46
(© Iakov Filimonov); © Spectrum Photofile: pp. 22 (© Ottmar
Bierwagen), 29 (© Ottmar Bierwagen); © SuperStock: p. 36
(© David Forbert).

Cover photograph reproduced with permission of National
Geographic Stock/© JAMES P. BLAIR.

We would like to thank Sarah Blue for her invaluable help in the
preparation of this book.

Every effort has been made to contact copyright holders of
any material reproduced in this book. Any omissions will
be rectified in subsequent printings if notice is given to the
publisher.

Contents

Some words in the book are in bold, **like this**. You can find out what they mean by looking in the glossary.

Introducing Haiti

The people of Haiti have always been different from their neighbours in the Caribbean. They speak French and **Creole**, while most of their neighbours speak Spanish or English. They practice Christianity and *vodou*, a religion with African roots. Their music also reflects ties with Africa. Most Haitians are **descendants** of slaves brought to Haiti from Africa in the 1600s. They fought for and won their independence in 1804. This made Haiti the first black **republic** in the world.

Where is Haiti?

Haiti occupies the western third of the island of Hispaniola. It is located between the Caribbean Sea and the North Atlantic Ocean. The Dominican Republic shares the island and forms Haiti's eastern border. Haiti has a total area of 27,750 square kilometres (10,714 square miles).

Earthquake in 2010

On 12 January 2010, Haiti suffered a massive earthquake. This shattering event killed more than 230,000 people, injured 300,000, and left 1.5 million people homeless. The earthquake focused world attention on this poor island nation, but there is much more to Haiti.

ROSE-ANNE AUGUSTE (BORN 1963)

Rose-Anne Auguste, born in Haiti in 1963, has spent her life helping Haitian women. In 1992 she opened the Women's Health Clinic in the capital, Port-au-Prince. Today she heads APROSIFA, an organization that provides support for women and girls who are the victims of violence.

Rocky cliffs overlook Haiti's coastline.

History: first black republic

The sea has always played a major role in Haiti's history. In about 2600 BC, the first people rowed to the island of Hispaniola in canoes. They were probably fishermen from South America. The Salanoids, who came from present-day Venezuela, arrived 2,000 years later. **Archeologists** have found examples of their pottery throughout Cuba, Jamaica, and Hispaniola, but no permanent settlements.

The last native people to reach Haiti were the Taínos, who came from Venezuela around AD 700. The population increased until 1490. These people were hard-working farmers who grew root vegetables all year round. They named the island *Ayti*, or *Hayti*, which means "mountainous".

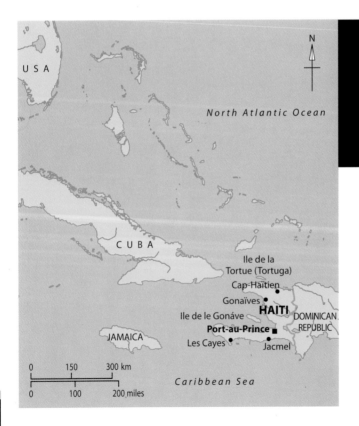

This map shows Haiti and its borders: the North Atlantic Ocean, the Caribbean Sea, and the Dominican Republic.

Columbus arrives

The explorer Christopher Columbus reached Hispaniola in 1492 and claimed the land for Spain. The Taínos were forced into **slave labour**, mining gold. Brutal working conditions and European diseases such as **smallpox** wiped out almost all these native people. By 1502, with few native slaves left, the Spanish began **importing** slaves from Africa.

The French take over

By 1640 French settlers had taken over the western portion of Hispaniola (now Haiti). The Spanish, who lost interest once the gold ran out, gave the land to the French in 1697. The French called Haiti Saint-Domingue. Between 1501 and 1803, Spanish and French settlers brought 772,734 African slaves to work in the huge coffee and sugar **plantations**. The 25,000 French settlers grew wealthy and powerful off the slaves' labour.

Thousands of Taíno people lived in coastal areas of Hispaniola when Christopher Columbus arrived in 1492.

Rebellion!

Free people of mixed black and white parentage, called **mulattoes**, could own land in Haiti, but they could not hold political office or work as teachers, doctors, or lawyers. In 1791 mulattoes rebelled against the French.

At about the same time, slave leaders met secretly and vowed to fight for their freedom. A brilliant slave named Toussaint l'Ouverture led the Haitian Revolution against the French. Revolt spread. After several years of fighting, l'Ouverture gained control of the entire island.

Toussaint l'Ouverture became a symbol of hope for slaves everywhere.

TOUSSAINT L'OUVERTURE
(AROUND 1743-1803)

Toussaint l'Ouverture, born near Cap-Haïtien, led the slave revolt against British, Spanish, and French armies. After he freed the slaves, he became "Governor for Life". In 1803 Emperor Napoleon of France kidnapped and imprisoned him. L'Ouverture died in a French prison later that year.

An independent Haiti

Jean-Jacques Dessalines became the first governor of an independent Haiti on 1 January 1804. Haiti became the first black **republic** and the second nation in the Western Hemisphere to become independent from a European power. The United States was the first.

Mulattoes	30,000	5.8%
Whites	40,000	7.7%
Slaves	450,000	86.5%

This chart shows the population of Saint-Domingue in 1791.

The Citadelle, which overlooks the Atlantic Ocean, was built in 1805 to protect against French attack.

Unstable government

After independence, powerful **dictators** ruled Haiti. They often used violence to gain and hold power. Between 1912 and 1915 six Haitian presidents were killed in office. For 19 years, from 1915, the United States entered Haiti and **occupied** the country in an attempt to restore order.

Throughout the 1900s, Haiti had leadership problems. In 1957 a dictator named Francois Duvalier, nicknamed "Papa Doc", took over. He used violence against anyone who disagreed with him. When Duvalier died in 1971, his 19-year-old son, nicknamed "Baby Doc", took over. He ruled until 1986 when he was overthrown. Then he escaped to France.

In 1990 Haiti held free elections, but the military overthrew the elected president, Jean-Bertrand Aristide. Because of continued problems in Haiti, the **United Nations** sent troops to help maintain order.

Living in Haiti now

By 2010 over 9 million people lived in Haiti. Today, the greatest challenge for Haiti and its people is recovering from the 2010 earthquake. Twenty-eight of the twenty-nine government buildings in the capital Port-au-Prince were destroyed. Thousands of government workers were killed. Others lost homes and families. The United Nations appointed former US president Bill Clinton as a special **envoy** to Haiti. Countries throughout the world pledged a total of £3.34 billion in donations to help Haiti's recovery.

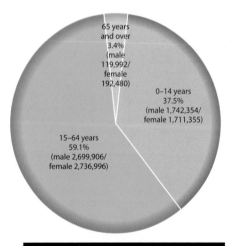

65 years and over
3.4%
(male 119,992/
female 192,480)

0–14 years
37.5%
(male 1,742,354/
female 1,711,355)

15–64 years
59.1%
(male 2,699,906/
female 2,736,996)

This graph shows the age spread of the Haitian population.

The earthquake damaged the National Palace in Port-au-Prince, home of Haiti's president. For months afterwards, the government operated out of tents behind the National Palace.

How to say...

	Creole	French
flag	*drapo*	*drapeau*
president	*prezidan*	*président*
government	*gouvènman*	*gouvernement*

Regions and resources: a land in danger

Mountains cover nearly 80 per cent of Haiti. Originally, forests covered the mountains, but today less than 2 per cent of Haiti is forested. Spanish and French **colonists** cut down trees to make room for sugar and coffee **plantations**. Later, logging companies cut timber for **export** to Europe and the United States.

Daily life

In farming areas, families often share a private yard surrounded by a big fence. The yard may include several two-room mud houses. It also includes a cooking area, a small garden to grow food, and pets. Before entering a yard, a visitor shouts "*Onè*" (honour), and the host replies "*Respè*" (respect).

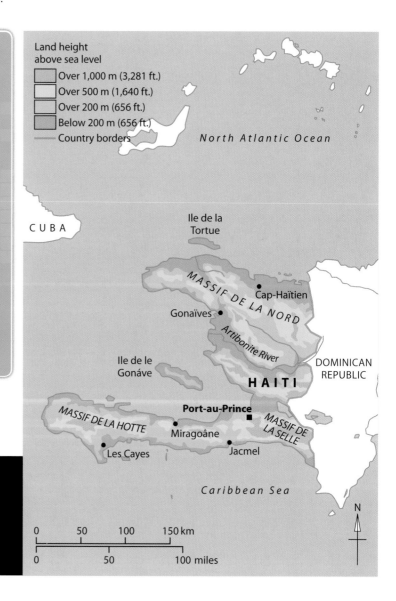

Land height above sea level
- Over 1,000 m (3,281 ft.)
- Over 500 m (1,640 ft.)
- Over 200 m (656 ft.)
- Below 200 m (656 ft.)
- Country borders

North Atlantic Ocean

CUBA

Ile de la Tortue

MASSIF DE LA NORD

Cap-Haïtien

Gonaïves

Artibonite River

Ile de le Gonáve

DOMINICAN REPUBLIC

HAITI

Port-au-Prince

MASSIF DE LA HOTTE

MASSIF DE LA SELLE

Miragoâne

Les Cayes

Jacmel

Caribbean Sea

N

0   50   100   150 km

0   50   100 miles

This map shows the land height and main natural features of Haiti.

This Haitian farmer is planting rice in a flooded paddyfield.

Haitians continue to destroy the forests. They use wood to cook and to make charcoal to sell to city dwellers. The loss of trees has led to flooding and mudslides. In February 2010, heavy rains caused a mudslide in Cap-Haïtien, Haiti's second largest city. It killed four children and injured two others.

Farmlands

Most Haitians are farmers. Haiti's largest farms grow coffee, mangoes, sugarcane, rice, and corn on the plains between mountains. These crops are taken to port cities, such as Port-au-Prince, for export to the United States, the Dominican Republic, and Canada.

Small farms are scattered throughout Haiti's steep and rugged terrain. Most farmers grow food for their families. They sell any surplus in the village markets. In February 2010, worried about food shortages, the government began providing farmers with better quality seeds and supplies.

The weather

Haiti has a **tropical** climate. In the capital of Port-au-Prince, temperatures average between 31 °Celsius (88 °Fahrenheit) in January and 35 °Celsius (95 °Fahrenheit) in July. In the mountains, the temperatures may dip to 10 °Celsius (50 °Fahrenheit). Haiti's first rainy season is from April to late June. The second occurs during October and November. The heaviest rains occur along the southern **peninsula** and in the northern plains and mountains.

Many of Haiti's 100 streams and rivers overflow when it rains, and then dry up during dry seasons. Even Haiti's longest river, the Arbonite River, which is normally more than 3 metres (10 feet) deep, dries up between rainy seasons.

Hurricanes and floods

Hurricane season is from June to September. Hurricane **storm surges** push seawater on to land causing flooding. In 2004 the floods from Hurricane Jeanne killed over 3,000 Haitians. In 2008 four hurricanes hit Haiti. Nearly 600 people were injured, around 1,100 died or disappeared, and 70 per cent of Haiti's crops were destroyed. In the months that followed, starvation killed many more, especially children.

How to say...

	Creole	French
rain	*lapli*	*pluie*
sun	*sole*	*soleil*
wind	*van*	*vent*

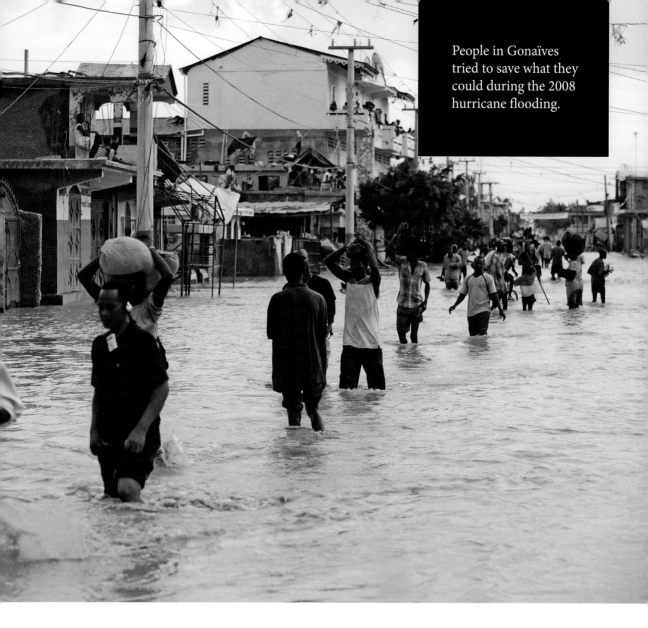

People in Gonaïves tried to save what they could during the 2008 hurricane flooding.

The 2010 earthquake

On 12 January 2010, at 4.53 p.m. a major earthquake struck Haiti. Scientists estimated that the earthquake had a **magnitude** of 7 on the **Richter Scale**, a system used to measure earthquakes. (Most earthquakes are 2.5 or less.) It was the most powerful earthquake to strike Haiti in 200 years. In the two weeks immediately after the main earthquake, more than 50 **aftershocks** struck the area. These may continue for several years.

Rushing to help

The earthquake struck about 20 kilometres southwest of Port-au-Prince. It produced violent shaking over a large area. In addition to Port-au-Prince and its suburbs, the cities of Grand-Goâve, Jacmel, Léogâne, Miragoâne, and Petit-Goâve also suffered heavy damage. Poorly built homes and buildings collapsed.

Rescue teams rushed to Haiti from Cuba, the Dominican Republic, Europe, the United States, and Venezuela. During the first 24 hours, rescue workers from the Dominican Republic pulled 17 people from the ruins. Relief workers and medical teams set up emergency hospitals and distributed food and water. **Cholera** and other diseases threaten survivors. People living in crowded conditions and without safe food and water became ill and died in the months after the earthquake.

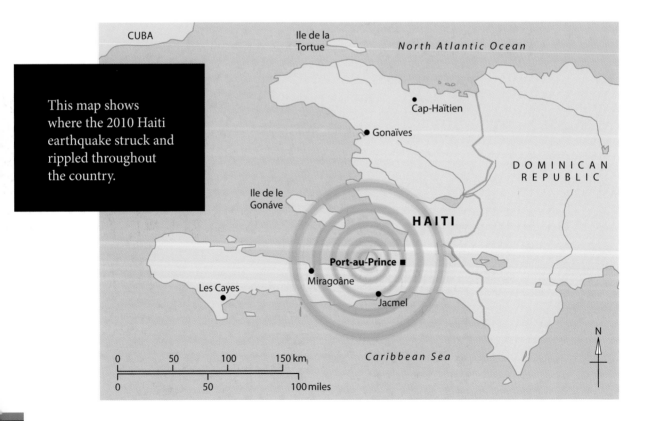

This map shows where the 2010 Haiti earthquake struck and rippled throughout the country.

Recovering from disaster

It will take Haiti years to recover from the earthquake. Months afterwards, people were still living in tents. By June 2010, engineers had tested 170,000 damaged buildings. They declared half of them unsafe and marked them for destruction. Experts say it will take 1,000 trucks working every day for three to five years to remove all the **debris** from the damaged buildings. But so far, only 300 lorries are available for the job.

These children live in an orphanage in Port-au-Prince.

Wildlife:
unusual creatures

Haiti is home to some fascinating creatures – tarantulas, iguanas, and scorpions. Scorpions live in lowland areas and have a poisonous sting. The Haitian brown tarantula eats insects, birds, lizards, and small mammals, but cannot kill humans.

The Haitian solenodon

Before Columbus, Haiti was home to many mammals. Most are now extinct. The Haitian solenodon is one of the few remaining native mammals. It has a long snout, large ears, and tiny eyes. It hunts at night and sleeps curled together with others in a cave, rock crevice, or hollow log.

Birds, sea life, and plants

Parrots and woodpeckers are common in Haiti. So are colonies of American flamingoes that stand 90 to 150 centimetres (3 to 5 feet) tall. Four types of turtles, spiny lobsters, red snappers, edible stingrays, and **tarpon** swim along Haiti's coast. Haiti has over 5,000 species of plants. These include many kinds of ferns and orchids. Fruit trees loaded with mangoes, coconuts, avocados, and grapefruit grow in populated areas.

The Haitian solenodon eats snails and oranges.

National parks

Haiti has four national parks. But with all of Haiti's other needs, they struggle to survive. Two parks include **cloud forests** which are home to many species of plants, insects, and birds.

Name	Location (see the map below)	Features
Parc Nacional Forêt des Pins	Far eastern mountains near Dominican border	Pine forest
Parc Nacional la Visite	Western section of Massif de la Selle mountain range	Mountains, cloud forest, waterfalls, limestone caves
Parc Nacional Macaya	Western end of southern peninsula	Cloud forest
Park Nacional Historique La Citadelle	Near Cap-Haïtien	The Citadel (see page 9)

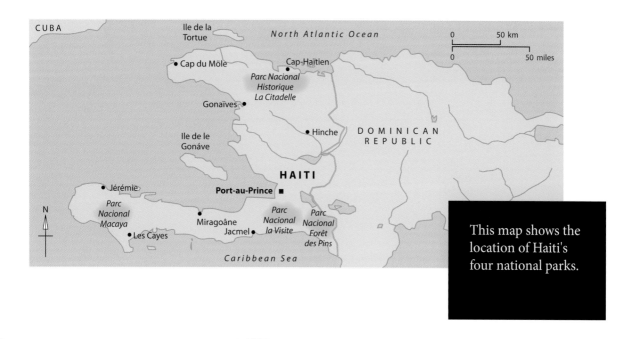

This map shows the location of Haiti's four national parks.

Infrastructure:
much still to do

Haiti is a **republic**. The people elect the president for a five-year term. The president appoints a **prime minister** who chooses a team of advisers. There is a National Assembly (30 members) and a Chamber of Deputies (99 members). After a **military coup** in 2004, the **United Nations** sent **peacekeepers** to Haiti to restore order. They also helped with the recovery after the 2010 earthquake. Haiti's government has many problems.

Unsafe water

In most countries, the government provides clean drinking water. In Haiti only 45 per cent of the people have clean water for drinking and cooking. Most people in rural areas use water from rivers and streams that often contains human and animal waste. Drinking this unclean water can cause children and babies to die of diseases.

This chart compares statistics for Haiti, the Dominican Republic, and the UK. Years of unstable government have left Haiti far poorer than its neighbour on Hispaniola.

	Haiti	Dominican Republic	United Kingdom
Population	9,876,000 (2007 figures)	9,953,000 (2007 figures)	61,281,806 (2010 estimate)
Literacy	62%	89%	99%
Annual income per person	£416	£2, 760	£22,132
Life expectancy	61 years	73 years	79 years
HIV/AIDS rate	2.2%	1.1%	0.2%

Healthcare

Before the earthquake, 60 per cent of Haiti's people had no healthcare services. According to 2009 World Health Organization statistics, Haiti has one nurse and three doctors for every 10,000 people. More babies, children under five, and pregnant women die in Haiti than in any other nation in the Western Hemisphere. The World Health Organization ranks Haiti's healthcare system as 138 out of 190 nations.

HIV/AIDS, a disease that makes it difficult to fight infections, is a major problem in Haiti. In 2007 about 120,000 people in Haiti were living with HIV. They will need good healthcare and medicines to survive. Haiti still needs to develop an education programme that teaches people how to avoid getting HIV.

This hospital in a suburb of Port-au-Prince treats poor children.

A troubled economy

Haiti is the poorest country in the Western Hemisphere. Two-thirds of Haitians live on small farms, growing only enough to supply their own needs. Before the earthquake, 80 per cent of Haiti's people lived below the **poverty line**. More than two-thirds of Haiti's people are unemployed. Factories in Port-au-Prince that produced clothes, sports goods, and electronic parts were destroyed in the earthquake. Before the earthquake, manufacturing accounted for about 20 per cent of Haiti's economy. After the earthquake, 500,000 people left Port-au-Prince to live with family in rural areas.

Haiti's currency is the gourde.

MYRIAM MERLET (1953-2010)

Myriam Merlet was a women's rights leader who headed Haiti's Ministry of Women. She founded Enfofamn to defend women's rights and to promote women's accomplishments. One of her projects was to re-name streets after Haitian women. She died in the 2010 earthquake.

Women and girls

Haitian poverty puts women and girls at high risk. **Domestic violence** is a problem in Haiti. After the earthquake, women's rights activists reported increased violence against women who were living in tents or other temporary housing.

Although the 1957 Constitution gave Haitian women the right to vote, they continue to fight for equal rights. Women's rights leaders work to reduce violence against women. They also try to promote equal opportunities for women in the home and workplace.

Haitian women often use their heads to carry loads to market.

City life

In 2008, 47 per cent of Haiti's people lived in cities. In the cities, wealthy people live in elegant homes with electricity and running water. The rest of the people, mostly extremely poor, live in rows of mud-and-brick huts or tiny tin shacks. They have no electricity, no safe drinking water, and no toilets. When it rains, water pours down the hillsides into these neighbourhoods causing disease and sometimes death.

Rural life

Most country dwellers are **peasants**. Many own or rent a small plot of land and a two-room wooden or mud house with a garden of beans, corn, and bananas. Men work as farmers or fishermen. The women care for the home and children. Cooking usually takes place outside over wood or charcoal fires. Electricity is rare.

These huts have adobe walls and thatched roofs.

Transportation

It is not easy to get around Haiti. There is no railway and 75 per cent of the roads are not paved. People use the local buses (called "tap-taps"), trucks, bicycles, and mules to travel and transport goods from place to place.

Colourful buses called "tap-taps" carry passengers throughout Haiti.

Daily life

Poverty is hardest on the children of Haiti. Before the earthquake, between 300,000 and 350,000 Haitian children lived in orphanages. Many were left there by parents too poor to care for them. Other children are forced to work long hours for little or no wages. The United Nations is working to combat child labour in Haiti. They are concerned that children will take dangerous construction jobs as part of the rebuilding work after the 2010 earthquake.

Education

State schools are free in Haiti. Children between the ages of 6 and 12 are required to attend. However, there are not enough schools or teachers. Only about one-third of Haitian children attend school. Many drop out before finishing primary school. Unfortunately, the 2010 earthquake destroyed about 90 per cent of the schools in Port-au-Prince and 40 per cent in the southern city of Jacmel. Rebuilding will take time.

Only about one-fifth of Haiti's children attend secondary school. Many leave school to help support their families. They may return later to finish their schooling. It is not unusual to see 20-year-old students in secondary school. Even so, only about half of Haitian adults can read and write.

Daily life

Creole is a mix of French and the West African languages spoken by Haitian slaves. Creole includes words from the Taíno people who lived in Haiti before the Spanish, as well as some Spanish, English, and Portuguese words. Most children in Haiti speak Creole, but school lessons are taught in French. Written Creole is not used in school.

Children as servants

About 300,000 children in Haiti are **restaveks**. In Creole *restavek* means "to stay with". Poor parents send children, especially girls ages 9 to 15, to stay with richer families. In exchange for food, shelter, and education, the children cook, carry water, clean the house, and do the laundry. They work long hours. Few attend school, and many are abused. Experts consider this a form of child slavery and they are working to end it.

Haiti's schools are often
crowded and short of supplies.

Culture: blending French and African

About 80 per cent of Haitians are **Roman Catholic**. Another 16 per cent are Protestants. Haitians celebrate the Christian holidays. **Carnival** begins in late January or early February and lasts several days and nights. Towns and cities hold parades with floats, bands, and dancers. People dress in bright colours and party late into the night. Carnival is followed by a forty-day period of reflection (Lent) until Easter when there are more joyous celebrations.

Recognizing *vodou*

Haiti's 1987 Constitution granted all Haitians religious freedom. For years the Catholic Church banned the practice of ***vodou*** (also spelled voodoo), a folk religion with African roots that often involves belief in magic. However, roughly half of Haiti's people, including many Christians, participate in some *vodou* practices. In 2003 President Jean-Bertrand Aristide officially recognized *vodou* as a religion.

These women practice both *vodou* and the Christian faith as they dance at Easter.

This is a painting by Hector Hyppolite.

Art

Haitian baskets, pottery, puppets, masks, and flags are sold at markets around the world. Haiti's artists produce colourful scenes of daily life in a simple style. Haitian art is on display in museums around the world.

Unfortunately, as a result of the 2010 earthquake, as many as 10,000 paintings and sculptures were buried in the ruins of the Musée d'Art Nader. Some of the items were very old. Others were modern works by famous Haitian artists such as Hector Hyppolite.

Haitian artists are also known for their **murals**. A series of murals painted on the walls of the Episcopal Holy Trinity Cathedral in Port-au-Prince showed Bible scenes. Many crumbled in the earthquake, but experts may be able to save at least four.

Music

People throughout Haiti enjoy singing and dancing. Much of Haiti's music contains African rhythms. People often make instruments, especially drums, from available materials. *Rara* bands perform music that has *vodou* roots and uses drum beats and songs brought from Africa. Bamboo and tin trumpets play one low note. Drums, **maracas**, and metal scrapers complete the band. *Racines* music combines jazz with *vodou* rhythms. Electric guitars, keyboards, and singing combine with the drums for a unique sound.

This woman is selling pork at a market stand.

Food

Food is an important part of every celebration. Haitian cooking mixes French and African dishes in a unique way. Haitians eat corn, rice, beans, and tropical fruits such as pineapple, mangoes, oranges, and grapefruit.

For breakfast, Haitians often have bread, butter, and coffee. Even children drink coffee. Lunch is the biggest meal of the day. It might be rice and beans with a salad of watercress and tomatoes.

Griot

Griot is one of Haiti's most popular dishes. This recipe serves six.

Ingredients:

- 1 kilogram shoulder of pork, cut into 2 centimetre cubes
- 1 finely chopped large onion
- 50 grams of chopped shallots
- 240 millilitres of orange juice
- 1 chopped hot green pepper
- 120 millilitres of vegetable oil
- salt, pepper, and a little thyme

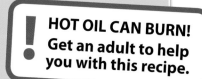

! HOT OIL CAN BURN! Get an adult to help you with this recipe.

Preparation:

Put all ingredients, except for the oil, in a large pot and marinate (soak) overnight in the fridge. Place the marinated pork on the stove, add water to cover all ingredients and simmer for 90 minutes. Once cooked, drain the mixture, add oil and fry the pork in the pot until brown and crusty on the outside, but tender on the inside.

Sports

Football, called *foútbol*, is the most popular sport in Haiti. Teams play on the street and in farmyards. Many city football pitches and stadiums were used as sites for temporary houses, schools, or hospitals after the 2010 earthquake. Even so, kids found ways to play *foútbol*. **Cockfighting** is also popular. Every town has a cockfighting pit. Owners pay for their cockerels to compete. Then, everyone bets on which cockerel will win the fight.

Television, radio, and the Internet

In 2009 Haiti had 94 radio stations and 7 television stations. Most people do not have televisions because they do not have electricity, but even poor farms have a radio that uses batteries. The telephone service in Haiti is amongst the least developed in Latin America or the Caribbean. Lack of a good phone service also makes Internet communication difficult. Haiti ranks 221 out of 232 nations in providing Internet services.

Literature

In the past, most Haitian novels and poems were written in French. However, in 1975 Frankétienne wrote his novel, *Dézafi*, in Creole. Now, many poets also write in Creole. Haitians who live overseas continue to write about Haiti, often discussing their guilt about leaving their beloved homeland.

Daily life

Children in Haiti, like kids everywhere, love to play. Boys play marbles, and girls play a game called rocks and bones, which is like jacks. They toss a stone into the air and gather as many sticks as possible before it lands. Young girls play with dolls, and boys play with toy cars and lorries. Often these toys are homemade.

Haitian kids play *foútbol* wherever they can find space.

Haiti today

About one in eight Haitians lives abroad. Many left for political reasons. Others left to find jobs and escape the extreme poverty. Most Haitians in the United States live in New York City or the southern state of Florida. In Canada, French-speaking Quebec also has a number of Haitian **immigrants**, as does the Dominican Republic.

Many hope to return to Haiti one day. They celebrate Haitian holidays, eat Haitian foods, and send money home. This money is often crucial to their families in Haiti. Many, such as hip-hop singer Wyclef Jean, have supported fund-raisers to help relieve the poverty in Haiti.

Rich in spirit

Today, the people of Haiti still struggle with inefficient government, extreme poverty, and natural disasters such as **hurricanes** and the 2010 earthquake. Even so, they find ways to celebrate life. They flavour their food with hot spices, their paintings with bright colours, and their get-togethers with music and dance. Haitians enjoy storytelling. After all, they live in a fascinating country with a story all of its own.

Daily life
When children gather to hear a storyteller in Haiti, the storyteller begins by asking, "*Cric?*" If they want to hear a story, they eagerly shout, "*Crac!*" and the story begins.

WYCLEF JEAN (BORN 1969)

Award winning hip-hop singer Wyclef Jean was born in Haiti. He moved to the United States at age 10. He says, "I'm proud to be Haitian. I represent Haiti in everything that I do". He felt that the country needed a new start to recover from the 2010 earthquake. He hoped to run for presidency but was not allowed to do so.

Fact file

Official name: Republic of Haiti

Nationality: Haitian

Location: Caribbean, western one-third of the island of Hispaniola, between the Caribbean Sea and the North Atlantic Ocean, west of the Dominican Republic

Capital: Port-au-Prince

Largest cities: Port-au-Prince (population 875,978)
Carrefour (population 430,250)
Delmas (population 359,451)

Total area: 27,750 square kilometres (10,714 square miles)

Bordering countries: Dominican Republic to the east

System of government: Republic

Date of constitution: approved March 1987

Many Haitians enjoy music and dance.

Date of independence: 1 January 1804 (from France)

Climate: tropical

Rainfall: Varies from a high of 1,950 millimetres (77 inches) in northern mountains to 500 millimetres (20 inches) along west coast

Coastline: 1,771 kilometres (1,100 miles)

Longest river: Arbonite River – 400 kilometres (249 miles)

Highest point: Morne La Selle – 2,680 kilometres (8,800 feet)

Lowest point: Caribbean Sea (sea level) – 0 metres (0 feet)

Terrain: mostly rough and mountainous

Agriculture products: coffee, mangoes, sugarcane, rice, corn, wood

Major industries: sugar refining, flour milling, textiles, cement, light assembly based on imported parts

Exports: clothing, manufacturing, oils, cocoa, mangoes, coffee

Major export markets: US 70%, Dominican Republic 8.8%, Canada 3%

Imports: food, manufactured goods, machinery, and transport equipment, fuels, raw materials

Major suppliers: US 34.2%, Dominican Republic 23.3%, China 4.5% (2008)

Population: 9,035,536 million (July 2009 estimate)

Languages: French and Creole

Local currency: gourde

Life expectancy: 61.38 years

Literacy rate: 52.9%

Official religion: Roman Catholic 80%, Protestant 16% (Baptist 10%, Pentecostal 4%, Adventist 1%, other 1%), none 1%, other 3%. Roughly half of the population practices *vodou*.

National coat of arms: Features a palm tree in the centre with red and blue flags tilting upward from the base. Two yellow cannons, cannonballs, a drum, and a ship's anchor complete the picture.

National motto: L'Union Fait la Force (In Union there is Strength)

National tree: Palm

National flower: Hibiscus

International memberships: United Nations, UNESCO, Organization of American States, and many others

Holidays:

1 January	Independence Day
2 January	Ancestors' Day
1 May	Agriculture and Labour Day
18 May	Flag Day
18 November	Battle of Vertières' Day

National anthem: "La Dessalinienne", written in 1903, honours
Haiti's first president, Jean-Jacques Dessalines

For our country, for our forefathers,
United let us march.
Let there be no traitors in our ranks!
Let us be masters of our soil.
United let us march, for our country,
For our forefathers.
For our forebears, for our country, let us toil joyfully.
May the fields be fertile, and our souls take courage.
Let us toil joyfully, for our forebears, for our country.
For our country, and for our forefathers, let us train our sons.
Free, strong, and prosperous, we shall always be as brothers.
Let us train our sons, for our country, and for our forefathers.
For our forebears, for our country, Oh God of the valiant!
Take our rights and our life, under your infinite protection,
Oh God of the valiant!
For our forebears, for our country.
For the flag, for our country, to die is a fine thing!
Our past cries out to us: Have a strong soul!
To die is a fine thing, for the flag, for our country.

Famous Haitians:

Jean-Bertrand Aristide (born 1953), former president
  (1991, 1994–1996, 2001–2004)
Rose Anne Auguste (born 1963), women's rights leader
Edwidge Danticat (born 1969), writer
Francois Duvalier (1907–1971), dictator
Hector Hyppolite (1894–1948), artist
Myriam Merlet (1953–2010), women's rights leader
Toussaint l'Overture (1743–1803), leader of slave revolt
Wyclef Jean (born 1972), musician

Timeline

BC is short for "before Christ". BC is added after a date and means that the date occurred before the birth of Jesus Christ, for example, 450 BC.

AD is short for *Anno Domini*, which is Latin for "in the year of our Lord". AD is added before a date and means that the date occurred after the birth of Jesus Christ, for example, AD 720.

2600 BC	First people arrive on Hispaniola from South America
600 BC	The Salanoids arrive from Venezuela
AD 700	Taínos reach Hispaniola from Venezuela
1492	Christopher Columbus arrives and names the island Hispaniola, which means "Little Spain"
1502	Spanish bring slaves from Africa
1625	French pirates occupy island of Tortuga
1697	Spain gives western part of Hispaniola to France. This becomes Haiti, or "Land of Mountains"
1801	A former black slave, Toussaint l'Ouverture, conquers Haiti, abolishing slavery and proclaiming himself governor-general over all Hispaniola
1804	Haiti becomes independent
1915	United States invades Haiti
1934	United States withdraws troops from Haiti, but maintains control of money matters until 1947
1956	Francois "Papa Doc" Duvalier seizes power and is elected president a year later

1971	Duvalier dies and is succeeded by his 19-year-old son, Jean-Claude, or "Baby Doc," who also declares himself president-for-life
1990	Jean-Bertrand Aristide is elected president
1991	Aristide is ousted in a coup; the United States and the Organization of American States intervene
1994	Aristide returns with support of US troops
1995	UN peacekeepers begin to replace US troops
1996	Rene Preval sworn in as president
2003	*Vodou* recognized as a religion
2004	Severe floods leave more than 2,000 dead or missing; UN peacekeepers help flood survivors; troops remain to help restore order
2008	Nearly 800 people are killed and hundreds are left injured as Haiti is hit by a series of devastating storms and hurricanes
2010	Tens of thousands of people are killed when a magnitude 7.0 earthquake hits the capital Port-au-Prince and its wider region – the worst earthquake in Haiti in over 200 years

Glossary

aftershock small earthquake or tremor that follows a major earthquake

AIDS (Acquired Immune Deficiency Syndrome) group of diseases caused by the HIV virus

archeologist person who studies past human life and culture by examining the physical remains, such as graves, tools, and pottery

Carnival celebrations that take place forty days before Easter, and are often observed with merrymaking and parades

cholera disease that is spread through unclean water. It can cause death within hours.

cloud forest high-altitude rainforest where mist is almost always present

cockfighting sport involving a fight between specially bred cockerels usually fitted with spurs

colonist person who creates a colony

Creole language spoken in Haiti that combines French, West African, and elements of other languages

debris ruins, rubble, or remains of something that is broken

descendant person whose roots can be traced back to a particular individual or group

dictator ruler with absolute power over the people

domestic violence acts of violence or abuse against a person living in one's household

envoy diplomat or representative

export ship goods to other countries for sale or exchange

HIV (Human Immunodeficiency Virus) virus that causes AIDS

hurricane violent tropical storm characterized by high winds and waves

immigrant person who moves from one country to another

import bring in from a foreign country for use or sale

magnitude measure of great size or amount

maraca dried gourd or a gourd-shaped rattle filled with seeds or pebbles to use as a rhythm instrument

military coup government takeover by a military group

mulatto person of mixed black and white parentage

mural large picture painted or affixed directly on a wall or ceiling

occupy to take possession or control of a place

peacekeeper person who maintains or restores peace

peasant small farmers or farm labourers of low social rank

peninsula portion of land that sticks out into water from the mainland

plantation place where coffee or sugar is grown

poverty line level at which one is classified as poor

prime minister head of the government

republic form of government in which a country is ruled by representatives elected by the people

restavek child who works as a household labourer in exchange for food, shelter, and education

Richter Scale scale, ranging from 1 to 10, used to indicate the intensity of an earthquake

Roman Catholic Christian church headed by the pope

slave labour work done by slaves without wages

smallpox highly contagious disease caused by a virus and often resulting in death

storm surge seawater pushed on to land by hurricane winds

tarpon large powerful fish with silvery scales that lives in warm Atlantic waters

tropical hot and humid

United Nations international organization formed in 1945 to promote world peace

vodou (also spelled voodoo) religion practiced in Haiti based on West African religions and some elements of Roman Catholic faith

Find out more

Books

Haiti: A Question and Answer Book, June Preszler (Capstone, 2007)

Haiti (The Caribbean Today), Bob Temple (Mason Crest, 2009)

Open the Door to Liberty!: A Biography of Toussaint L'Ouverture, Anne Rockwell
    (Harcourt, 2009)

Oxford Children's History of the World, Neil Grant
    (Oxford University Press, 2006)

The Earthquake in Haiti (Essential Events), Ann Lies (ABDO, 2010)

Websites

kids.yahoo.com/reference/world-factbook/country/ha--Haiti
This is the Yahoo World FactBook for Kids website for Haiti.

www.katw.org/pages/sitepage.cfm?id=154
The Kids Around the World website supplies information about the lives of
young people in various countries, including Haiti.

kids.nationalgeographic.com/kids/places/find/haiti
The National Geographic for Kids website is a source of information about
different countries. This is the link for Haiti.

www.plan-uk.org/rebuilding_haiti
The official website of Plan, a child-centred community development
organization. Find out about the work they are doing in Haiti to help the
victims of the earthquake.

Organizations to contact

Travel to Haiti has become extremely difficult since the 2010 earthquake, with many structures, including the airport, severely damaged or destroyed. But there are lots of organizations assisting Haiti recover and rebuild from the damage.

http://www.redcross.org.uk/About-us/News/2011/January/One-year-on-recovery-gives-Haiti-hope-for-the-future
The website of the British Red Cross. Find out about the work they have been doing to aid the recovery programme after the earthquake in Haiti.

www.habitat.org/intl/lac/89.aspx
Habitat for Humanity: This organization builds shelters for homeless people in Haiti.

www.doctorswithoutborders.org/news/article.cfm?id=4926&cat=field-news
Doctors Without Borders: See what this organization that provides free healthcare has been doing in Haiti.

www.yele.org
Yele Haiti: Wyclef Jean's non-profit organization.

Topic tools

You can use these topic tools for your school projects. Trace the map onto a sheet of paper, using the thick black outlines to guide you.

Haiti's flag was created on 18 May 1803. It has two equal bands of colour with the top blue and the bottom red. The coat of arms is in the centre. During the fight for independence from France, Jean-Jacques Dessalines ripped away the white band of the French flag, leaving only the blue and red stripes to show that Haiti no longer belonged to France. Copy the flag design and then colour in your picture. Make sure you use the right colours!

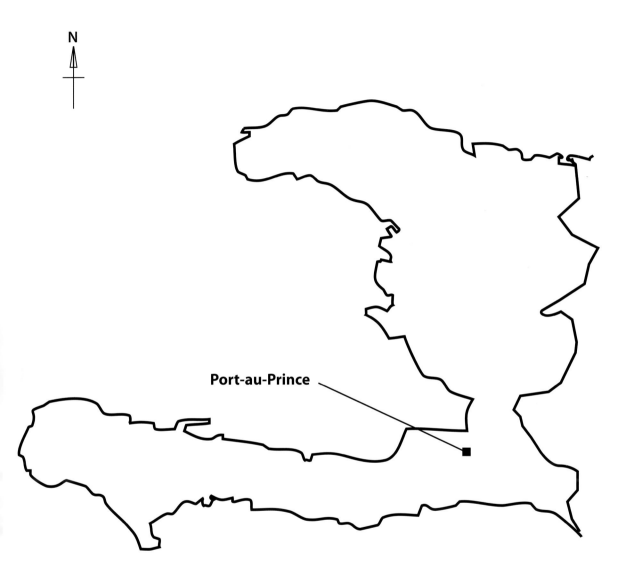

Port-au-Prince

Index

Titles in the series

Afghanistan	978 1 406 22778 9
Brazil	978 1 406 22785 7
Chile	978 1 406 22786 4
Costa Rica	978 1 406 22787 1
Cuba	978 1 406 22788 8
Czech Republic	978 1 406 22792 5
England	978 1 406 22799 4
Estonia	978 1 406 22793 2
France	978 1 406 22800 7
Germany	978 1 406 22801 4
Haiti	978 1 406 22789 5
Hungary	978 1 406 22794 9
India	978 1 406 22779 6
Iran	978 1 406 22780 2
Iraq	978 1 406 22781 9
Italy	978 1 406 22802 1
Latvia	978 1 406 22795 6
Lithuania	978 1 406 22796 3
Mexico	978 1 406 22790 1
Pakistan	978 1 406 22782 6
Poland	978 1 406 22797 0
Scotland	978 1 406 22803 8
Wales	978 1 406 22804 5
Yemen	978 1 406 22783 3